CHOMP!
Big Teeth

THIS EDITION
Editorial Management by Oriel Square
Produced for DK by WonderLab Group LLC
Jennifer Emmett, Erica Green, Kate Hale, *Founders*

Editors Grace Hill Smith, Libby Romero, Michaela Weglinski;
Photography Editors Kelley Miller, Annette Kiesow, Nicole DiMella;
Managing Editor Rachel Houghton; **Designers** Project Design Company;
Researcher Michelle Harris; **Copy Editor** Lori Merritt; **Indexer** Connie Binder; **Proofreader** Larry Shea;
Reading Specialist Dr. Jennifer Albro; **Curriculum Specialist** Elaine Larson

Published in the United States by DK Publishing
1745 Broadway, 20th Floor, New York, NY 10019

Copyright © 2023 Dorling Kindersley Limited
DK, a Division of Penguin Random House LLC
22 23 24 25 26 10 9 8 7 6 5 4 3 2 1
001-333864-May/2023

All rights reserved.
Without limiting the rights under the copyright reserved above, no part of this publication may be reproduced, stored in or introduced into a retrieval system, or transmitted, in any form, or by any means (electronic, mechanical, photocopying, recording, or otherwise), without the prior written permission of the copyright owner.
Published in Great Britain by Dorling Kindersley Limited

A catalog record for this book
is available from the Library of Congress.
HC ISBN: 978-0-7440-7117-7
PB ISBN: 978-0-7440-7118-4

DK books are available at special discounts when purchased in bulk for sales promotions, premiums, fundraising, or educational use. For details, contact: DK Publishing Special Markets,
1745 Broadway, 20th Floor, New York, NY 10019
SpecialSales@dk.com

Printed and bound in China

The publisher would like to thank the following for their kind permission to reproduce their images:
a=above; c=center; b=below; l=left; r=right; t=top; b/g=background

123RF.com: Andreas Meyer 31cl; **Alamy Stock Photo:** Blickwinkel / McPHOTO / E. u. H. Pum 27br, Blickwinkel / Mcphoto / Vlz 10-11, Images of Africa Photobank / Carla Signorini 26-27, Ernie Janes 9tr, Debbie Jolliff 30cra, Juniors Bildarchiv GmbH / Maier, R. / juniors@wildlife 30bc, Simon Litten 6cb, Nature Photographers Ltd / Ernie Janes 7tr, Wildlife / Robert McGouey 16br, 16-19, Rod Williams 6-7; **Dorling Kindersley:** Wildlife Heritage Foundation, Kent, UK 9bl, Jerry Young 22br, 31tl; **Dreamstime.com:** Unjhuz 17bc, Stephan Olivier 27bc, Planetfelicity 31bl, Stu Porter 23br, Ondřej Prosický 30cr, Lianquan Yu 31clb; **Getty Images:** DigitalVision / Paul Souders 25br, Manoj Shah 4cr; **Getty Images / iStock:** BELOW_SURFACE 19br, Howard Chen 18-19, GlobalP 3cb, Marcelauret 22-23, Rufous52 8-9, ShaneMyersPhoto 30, Siempreverde22 25br, slowmotiongli 11br, Yamtono_Sardi 11bl; **naturepl.com:** Eric Baccega 5br, Flip Nicklin 28-29, 29br; **Shutterstock.com:** BlueBarronPhoto 13b, Henk Bogaard 21bc, Neil Bromhall 14-15, 15br, Danita Delimont 17bl, Adalbert Dragon 4bl, Vlad G 5tr, Roger de la Harpe 20br, 20-21, Eric Isselee 9br, 21bl, Kelp Grizzly Photography 12-13, Mark_Kostich 4-5, David A Litman 13tr, Nathan Pang 12br, Martin Prochazkacz 19clb, M Rose 7bc, Craig Russell 10bc, Yunus Topal 24-25, wildestanimal 18crb

Cover images: *Front:* **Dreamstime.com:** Anastasiya Aheyeva c, Valerii Khadeiev, Inha Semiankova cl;
Back: **123RF.com:** skellos cra

All other images © Dorling Kindersley
For more information see: www.dkimages.com

For the curious
www.dk.com

CHOMP!
Big Teeth

Ruth A. Musgrave

Some teeth are big. Some are small. These teeth will make you smile.

5

These deer have two long teeth.

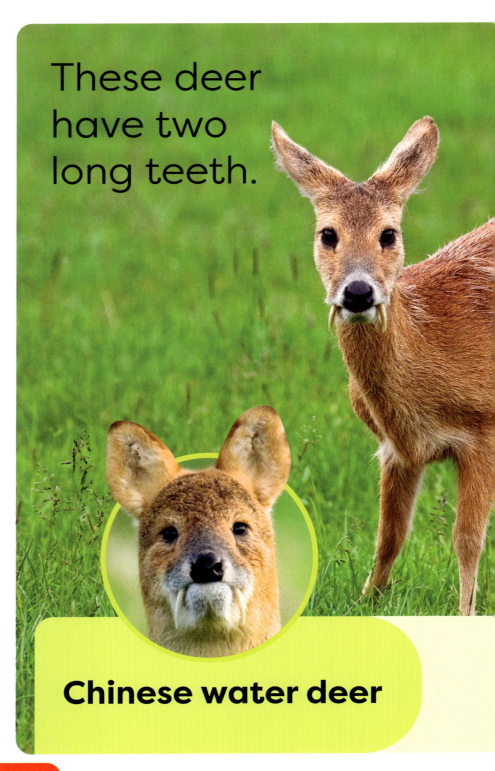

Chinese water deer

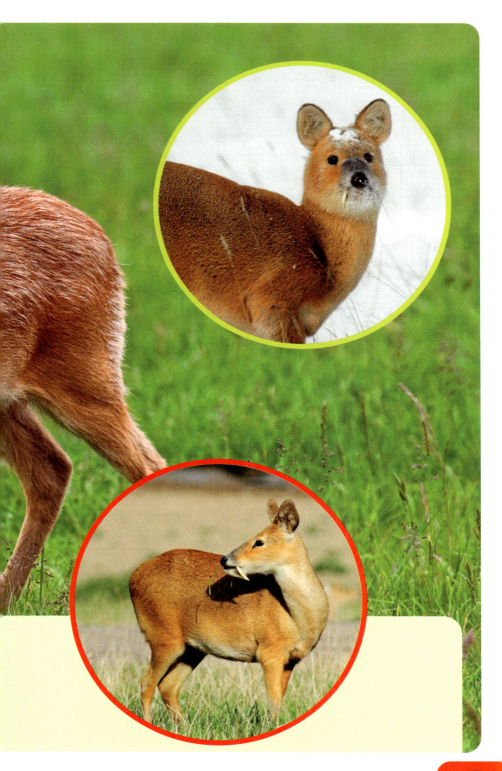

7

This big cat has sharp teeth.

clouded leopard

Look at how these teeth stick out!

babirusa
[BA-buh-roo-sa]

teeth

An otter opens shells with its teeth.
It eats the meat inside.

sea otter

This animal digs holes with its teeth.

naked mole rat

15

This animal cuts down trees. It makes a house with sticks.

beaver

This animal eats fish. It has many rows of teeth.

great white shark

Open wide!
Mom has big teeth.
Her baby will, too,
when it grows up.

hippopotamus

This animal grabs food with its teeth.

crocodile

23

This animal lives in the cold.
It uses its teeth to get out of the water.

walrus

These teeth can pull off tree bark.

elephant

This animal has the longest tooth of all.

narwhal
[NAR-wall]

29

Animals need teeth. They use them to eat and stay safe.
Now that's something to smile about.

Glossary

crocodile
an animal that lives in water

naked mole rat
an animal that digs and lives in the dirt

great white shark
a fish that lives in the ocean

hippopotamus
an animal that lives in the water and eats grass on land

narwhal
a whale that lives where it is cold

Quiz

Answer the questions to see what you have learned. Check your answers with an adult.

1. How does an otter use its teeth?
2. Which animal digs with its teeth?
3. Which animal has many rows of teeth?
4. Which animal pulls bark off a tree?
5. Which animal has the longest tooth?

1. To open shells 2. Naked mole rat 3. Great white shark
4. Elephant 5. Narwhal